CW01052170

On Statues

THE ERNEST JONES LECTURE 1995

JAMES FENTON

SYRENS

SYRENS Published by the Penguin Group. Penguin Books Ltd, 27 Wrights Lane, London w8 5TZ, England. Penguin Books USA Inc., 375 Hudson Street, New York, New York 10014, USA. Penguin Books Australia Ltd, Ringwood, Victoria, Australia. Penguin Books Canada Ltd, 10 Alcorn Avenue, Toronto, Ontario, Canada M4V 3B2. Penguin Books (NZ) Ltd, 182–190 Wairau Road, Auckland 10, New Zealand. Penguin Books Ltd, Registered Offices: Harmondsworth, Middlesex, England. Published in Syrens 1995. Set in 9.5/12pt Monotype Bembo by Datix International Limited, Bungay, Suffolk. Printed and bound by Page Bros., Norwich. 1 2 3 4 5 6 7 8 9 10

On Statues

In September 1938, Freud moved into his last home at 20 Maresfield Gardens, along with his collection of several hundred antique statuettes. How shocking, how hostile the previous sentence would be, if for 'antique statuettes' one substituted the phrase 'fluffy toys'. It's the fluffiness that would shock, though, the frivolity of it – not the idea that Freud had toys, and played with them all his life.

For how could such behaviour shock us, in a man known for his belief that happiness consists in the realization of a childhood wish? That was what made Schliemann happy, when he discovered Troy. This was the way Freud thought, and if Freud too found happiness among his statuettes, we can hardly be wrong in looking for some infantile component in this happiness.

Did he talk to his statuettes? Did they talk to him? Our metaphors are never far from such assertions, and Max Pollack's etching of 1914 seems to imply a dialogue between Freud and the objects on his desk.[1] Striking too is the fact that, whereas many a horror story has been based on the idea that a toy, a doll, comes to life and acquires a will of its own, Freud himself thought there was nothing uncanny in such an event. He found that 'in their early games children do not distinguish at all sharply between living and inanimate objects, and that they are especially fond of treating dolls like live people', and that 'children have no fear of their dolls coming to life, they may even desire it'.[2]

As for the idea that a marble sculpture might come to life – this is not only the theme of the essay on Jensen's *Gradiva*, it is also consciously evoked in the discussion of Michelangelo's *Moses*. 'How often', says Freud, 'have I mounted the steep steps from the unlovely Corso Cavour to the lonely piazza where the

1 Lynn Gammwell and Richard Wells (eds.) *Sigmund Freud and Art: His Personal Collection of Antiquities*, London, 1989, p. 152.
2 'The "Uncanny"', Penguin Freud Library, vol. 14, p. 355.

deserted church stands, and have essayed to support the angry scorn of the hero's glance! Sometimes I have crept cautiously out of the half-gloom of the interior as though I myself belonged to the mob upon whom his eye is turned – the mob which can hold no fast conviction, which has neither faith nor patience, and which rejoices when it has regained its illusory idols.'[3]

And the statue must come to life, because what Freud wants to know is: what was happening the moment before the moment depicted by the artist, and what will happen next? What was the hand doing with the beard? What will happen to the Tablets of the Law? And it seems that Freud thought that one day he would be given the answer to these questions, if he came cautiously upon the statue, and seized upon its living self, just as a child captures a limpet unawares, by stalking it on its rock.

That was the instinctive inquirer. You will recall that Ernest Jones, in whose honour this lecture is given, provided some scholarly evidence, a proof of Freud's hypothesis, when he sent a copy of the *Burlington Magazine* containing an illustration of a small bronze Moses in the Ashmolean Museum, then

3 'The Moses of Michelangelo', Penguin Freud Library, vol. 14, p. 255.

attributed to Nicholas of Verdun. And Freud was delighted that Jones had found a Moses that held its beard in the way that he surmised that Michelangelo's had been grasping its own, in that moment before the moment the artist chose. And the earlier, bronze Moses 'shows us an instant during his storm of feeling, while the statue in San Pietro in Vincoli depicts the calm when the storm is over'.[4]

So these statues are expected to serve in an inquiry into the mind and the emotions of Moses himself, and Freud stands before them in the role of the backsliding Hebrew. Surely if there can be life in such statues, there may be toys, speaking toys, among those several hundred statuettes; and it might well be that those who arranged Freud's possessions in Maresfield Gardens felt, as they set out the statuettes upon the desk, that they were making the old man happy, as one seeks to make a child at home by taking its dolls to the hospital bed. Statuette, doll, statue – they are not synonyms, but they belong to a family of meanings. Change the word a little, the whole sentence shifts to reveal new treasures of truth.

In September 1938, Freud moved into his last home at 20 Maresfield Gardens, along with his collection

4 'The Moses of Michelangelo', p. 282.

of several hundred *statues*. What an event that would have been! They would have had to pull down the neighbouring houses, and lay out new grounds to accommodate the collection. And if we had been standing near by as the old man arrived with his stone retinue, and if I had asked you who this Freud was, with his hundreds of statues, his thousands of antiquities, you would have been moved to make sense of it thus: this Freud is a foreign prince who has come here to die, and the statues have been brought for his tomb. And what you would have said would have been true, for these antiquities form both his memorial and his tomb – since they include the urn in which his ashes are buried, and since Maresfield Gardens is his mausoleum.

But if, with a final turn of the switch, one were to transform the sentence yet again, and say that Freud arrived in his last home with a collection of several hundred *colossi* – statues so huge that the whole triangle between Finchley Road and Fitzjohn's Avenue and, say, Frognal Lane, would have to be obliterated to accommodate them – and once again we were bystanders, and I asked you for your interpretation of the event, then I think you would say that this Freud must be a magus, and that the King of this country has invited him here and laid out these new avenues and set up these colossi, to protect this city and this country from its enemies.

And once again I must congratulate you on the grandeur of your interpretation which, while it seems grossly flattering to our monarchy, reflects something of the grandeur of Freud's own sense of purpose. 'After the destruction of the Temple in Jerusalem by Titus,' he wrote, 'Rabbi Jochanan ben Sakkai asked for permission to open a school at Jabneh for the study of the Torah. We are going to do the same. We are, after all, used to persecution by our history, tradition and some of us by personal experience . . .'[5]

And so we have Freud's permission, his encouragement, to compare the retinue moving into Maresfield Gardens with the Jewish people at the start of the diaspora, but with this difference — that Rabbi Jochanan ben Sakkai must have taken his books to Jabneh, but Freud's library had been sold. What Freud took into exile we might want to compare with the gods which Aeneas and his father carried from blazing Troy, were it not that, if we call these statuettes gods, we are in danger of walking straight

5 Ernest Jones, *Sigmund Freud: Life and Work*, 4th impression, London 1980, vol. 3, p. 236.

into the plate glass window of taboo. Freud can be a rabbi on his way to Jabneh, can be Moses leading his people to the promised land – but not with these heathen gods in tow, not with these falcon-headed images, these sphinxes, these idols of Amon-Re and the Baboon of Thoth.

Did Freud worship these images? Did he bow down before the Baboon of Thoth? We know already, because we have had his word for it, that when he comes before Michelangelo's Moses it is as a member of the mob, 'the mob which can hold no fast conviction, which has neither faith nor patience, and which rejoices when it has regained its illusory idols'. That is what we meant by calling him a backsliding Hebrew. It does not strike Freud as necessary to point out that the statue of Moses *itself* embodies an infringement of Mosaic Law, a particularly bold infringement if the statue is said to represent the moment at which Moses sees his people worshipping the Golden Calf. But this infringement is part of an age-old tradition, most vividly represented by a statue in Bern which shows Moses holding up the Tablets of the Law and pointing specifically to the second commandment:

Thou shalt not make unto thee any graven image, or any likeness of any thing that is in heaven above, or that is in the earth beneath, or that is in the water under the earth. Thou shalt not bow down thyself to them, nor serve them: for I the Lord thy God am a jealous God, visiting the iniquity of the fathers upon the children unto the third and fourth generation of them that hate me; and shewing mercy unto thousands of them that love me, and keep my commandments.[6]

You must not make any representational object, and you must not, having made such an object, venerate it in any way. No other art has been honoured with such a general taboo. No other art is of concern to the author of the Ten Commandments. That the fight between art and religion is an ancient and a necessary one we may concede, since all art tends to arrogate authority to itself, and all religion aspires to a monopoly on authority. But the arrogance of the other arts can be contained. Music can be put to good use. Poetry too has been set its tasks around the house of God. Even drama has been allowed to encroach, although always under profound suspicion. But the representational arts, and particularly that of sculpture, come with such a freight of heathenish memory, such a burden of idolatrous implication, that they have been banned outright . . .

6 Exodus 20: 4–6.

. . . and have won, piecemeal, their appeal against the ban. So we learn that some Jewish authorities 'interpret the second commandment as forbidding only those images made by a Jew for worship by a Jew, while at least one commentator asserts that the verse applies even to images a Jew might make for non-Jews to worship. Some take "sculpted" to mean incised as well as built up; others regard it as only three-dimensional. Some speak of "image" as referring to the human form; others see it as intending any form.' And some, apparently, have tolerated a painted profile, while maintaining a ban on the human face seen fully frontal.[7]

All of which is a tribute to the power of man's desire to represent, and to the ability of his mind to block out an inconvenient injunction – to interpret a text away. Freud was not at the head of a backsliding tradition – he was its heir. Jewish representational art, as seen in the old cemeteries of Europe, has a tradition dating back to the second century before Christ. The taboo had been well broken, and for long. But while Freud seems to have been happy to collect graven images (some of them, no doubt, of

7 Arnold Schwartzman, *Graven Images: Graphic Motifs of the Jewish Gravestone*, foreword by Chaim Potock, New York, 1993, p. 9.

precisely the type that the scriptural writers ab-
horred), he was not as insouciant about the taboo as
he seems in the essay on Michelangelo. At least, by
the time Freud reached London he had come to the
conclusion that the prohibition against worshipping
God in a visible form had had a profound effect
upon the Jews:

For it meant that a sensory perception was given second
place to what may be called an abstract idea – a triumph of
intellectuality over sensuality or, strictly speaking, an instinctual renunciation, with all its necessary consequences –

which were that

the individual's self-esteem is increased, that he is made
proud – so that he feels superior to other people who have
remained under the spell of sensuality. Moses, as we know,
conveyed to the Jews an exalted sense of being a chosen
people. The dematerialization of God brought a fresh and
valuable contribution to their secret treasure.[8]

But this passage leads straight into a reference to the
Jews' misfortunes, the destruction of the Temple
and, once again, the opening of the first Torah

8 'Moses and Monotheism', Penguin Freud Library, vol. 13, pp.
360, 362.

school in Jabneh. It is as if the prohibition had some part to play in those misfortunes, as well as in the strengths of the Jews. It is as if that instinctual renunciation had exacted a heavy price.

And among Christians too, the meaning of the second commandment was subverted, qualified or even reversed to accommodate a possible *duty* to venerate religious images, images which had found their place in worship at least by the time of the establishment of the Church under Constantine – so that there never was a post-classical world without statues and images that were revered. And some classical images were co-opted, as happened to Lysippus' statue of the resting Hercules, which stood in the hippodrome at Constantinople, but which was transformed by belief into Adam. The hero resting from his labours turned easily into the First Man sitting on a basket, contemplating the loss of Paradise – an image which spread throughout the Christian world in portable ivory form.

They were marvellous, those statues which survived being 'destroyed or toppled by the blessed Gregory' and which a certain Englishman, Master Gregorius, described in Rome in the thirteenth century. Of a Venus he says:

This image is made from Parian marble with such wonderful and intricate skill that she seems more like a living creature than a statue; indeed she seems to blush in her nakedness, a reddish tinge colouring her face, and it appears to those who take a close look that blood flows in her snowy complexion. Because of this wonderful image, and perhaps some magic spell that I'm unaware of, I was drawn back three times to look at it despite the fact that it was two stades distant from my inn.[9]

That possibility of enchantment, that sense of a statue possessing its own inner life – that could not be contemplated in those days with anything like Freud's equanimity, or a child's eagerness that a doll might come to life. Too much was at risk, too solemn a curse hung over the idolater. So that, in Ghiberti's *Commentaries* (written around 1450), we find an account of the discovery in Siena of a statue also signed by Lysippus, which caused such enthusiasm among the painters and sculptors and goldsmiths of the city that it was set up with great pomp, as the focus of a fountain. But after the city had suffered much in the wars with Florence, the flower of the citizenry came together in council, and it was pointed

9 Master Gregorius, *The Marvels of Rome*; see *Journal of Roman Studies* IX, 1919, p. 26.

out that everything had gone wrong since the discovery of the statue, that idolatry was forbidden to their faith, and that even if they buried the statue again on their own territory, their misfortunes would continue. So the statue was taken to Florentine territory, and reburied there.[10]

Such careful ratiocination, such concern for the eventual resting-place of the image – such has only rarely been the fate of these dangerous images. Much more typical, at times of iconoclasm, has been a blank, destructive rage, a desire to mutilate and humiliate the object of veneration, a scene such as we glimpse in this account of the destruction of the altarpiece at Sint-Jacobs in Ghent:

The chapel was unlocked (I do not know by what folly) and a lad of fourteen or fifteen came in broad daylight with an iron bar to smash, gouge, and otherwise damage the faces and hands of the little alabaster figures in the altarpiece. No one had the courage to stop even such youngsters (even though there were only one or two involved), because they were all astonished, and afraid that it was done at the behest of some powerful individual. No one knew what led him to commit this act.

10 Ghiberti, *I Commentarii*, ed. J. von Schlosser, Berlin, 1912, p. 63.

This was in the Low Countries, during the second wave of image-smashing in the 1560s, and a sense of that period comes pungently from the page. One child is out of control, smashing images which have hitherto been considered the treasures of the city: but everyone cowers indoors, afraid that something is afoot, some powerful individual has ordered this. It's not like cowering behind your front door as a mob smashes up the housing estate, knowing that the destruction is aimless and spontaneous. It's like knowing there is an important power shift in process, but having no clue as to what the shift might be – knowing only that at such times the people are helpless.

Or again, in Bruges during the French Revolution, we read that:

The heads of the statues taken from the Town Hall were brought to the market-place and smashed to pieces by people who were very angry and embittered. They also burned all traces of the hateful devices that had previously served the Old Law, such as gibbets, gallows and whips. Throughout these events the whole market square echoed to the constant cries of the assembled people: 'Long live the Nation! Long live Freedom!'[11]

11 John W. Steyaert, *Late Gothic Sculpture: The Burgundian Netherlands*, Ghent, 1994, p. 23.

How did the heads of statues from centuries before become implicated in the gallows and gibbets of the day? Their misfortune was to be available to a crowd in search of a symbolic action, a crowd like the soldiers who ravaged Canterbury Cathedral in 1642, who,

entering the church and choir, giant-like began a fight with God himself, overthrew the communion table, tore the velvet cloth from before it, defaced the goodly screen, or tabernacle-work, violated the monuments of the dead, spoiled the organs, broke down the ancient rails and seats, with the brazen eagle that did support the Bible, forced open the cupboards of the singing-men, rent some of their surplices, gowns and Bibles, and carried away others, mangled all our service-books, and the books of Common Prayer, bestrewing the whole pavement with the leaves thereof: a miserable spectacle to all good eyes. But as if this had been too little to satisfy the fury of some indiscreet zealots among then (for many did abhor what was done already) they further exercised their malice upon the arras hanging in the choir, representing the whole story of our Saviour; wherein observing divers figures of Christ (I tremble to express their blasphemies), one said, 'here is Christ', and swore that he would stab him: another said, 'here is Christ', and swore that he would rip up his bowels;

which they accordingly did, so far as the figures were capable thereof, besides many other villainies. And not content therewith, finding another statue of Christ in the frontispiece of the South-gate, they discharged against it forty shots at the least, triumphing much, when they did hit it in the head or face, as if they were resolved to crucify him again in his figure, whom they could not hurt in truth.

And Margaret Aston, who reprints this passage, comments that 'images were surrogates or dummies on which were vented some of the anger felt towards inaccessible human agents. Rage against the living might be discharged on images of the dead.'[12] But one supposes that rage against the dead came into the story as well, and that what began as pious rage turned into rage against Christ.

Generally speaking, religious iconoclasm has reserved a particular hatred for sculpture, rather than the painted or woven image, because it is sculpture that seems to be the target of Moses' wrath. And it is true of statues in general that they are vulnerable to, that they invite, mutilation: noses and hands get lopped off, suffering the punishment of thieves; the

12 Margaret Aston, *England's Iconoclasts: Laws Against Images*, Oxford, 1982, p. 62.

male genitals are a target, both for vandalism and for high-minded mutilation – all the erections of the Egyptian god Min seem to have been crudely censored; and heads, finally, are both physically vulnerable and a trophy, and can be valuable booty – as the thieves perhaps thought who sawed off the heads of Henry Moore's bronze king and queen in Scotland last year.

And statues are vulnerable when they are made of precious metals, and most metals are precious to someone, particularly in time of war. Where are most of the bronze casts of the greatest statues in Rome, which Primaticcio made for the King of France? Where are the great doors of Saint Denis? They are field-guns. They are the sons of guns, the grandsons of cannons. Who knows where they are? They have suffered so many reincarnations.

Ghiberti tells the following story:

In Germany in the city of Cologne lived a master much experienced in the art of sculpture, he was of the highest genius, his name was Gusmin; he was employed by the Duke of Anjou, who had him make a great many works in gold; among other works he made a golden altar and with all solicitude and care he executed this altar very excellently. He was perfect in his works, equal to the ancient Greek sculptors; he made the heads and all the nude parts marvellously well. There was no fault in him, save that his statues were somewhat squat. He was very outstanding and skilled and excellent in his art. I have seen many figures cast after his. He had the most delicate air to his works, he was very skilled. He saw the work destroyed that he had made with so much love and art on account of the public needs of the Duke; he saw his labour had been in vain and he fell upon his knees and raised up his eyes to Heaven saying: O Lord, O Lord, Thou who governest Heaven and Earth and has created all things; my ignorance be not so great that I follow anyone but thee, have mercy on me. Forthwith he undertook to give away whatever he owned for love of the Creator of all. He went up on a mountain where there was a great hermitage: he entered and did penance as long as he lived: he grew old, he died in the time of Pope Martin. Some young men who tried to gain knowledge of the art of sculpture told me how skilled he was in one art and another and how he painted where he was living; skilled he was and he died in the 438th Olympiad. He was a very great draughtsman and very gentle. Young men who desired to learn went to see him and when they begged him he received them most humbly, gave them skilled advice and showed them a great many proportions and made them many examples; he was most perfect. With great humility did he die in his hermitage.

Altogether he was most excellent and of a most saintly life.[13]

This story, this little hagiography, sounds like legend, but is most probably true. There probably was a sculptor called Gusmin, who would have worked for Louis I of Anjou, a great patron of goldsmiths, among whose inventories is listed a very large golden altar, *une très grande table d'autel d'or*, which was either sold or sent to the mint in 1381 in order to raise money for the conquest of the Kingdom of Naples. This war would be covered by the phrase, 'the public needs of the Duke'.

And it has been calculated that Gusmin would have been born around 1340 and would have worked for Louis from 1360 to the time of the destruction of his work two decades later. And as we see from the story, he took that destruction, that sudden complete loss of value, as a judgement against himself, and he spent the remaining forty years of his life in expiation of his sins. During those forty years, his reputation persisted among goldsmiths and sculptors (the two professions overlapped) and was kept alive by small casts after his work, which were probably not so

13 Richard Krautheimer, *Lorenzo Ghiberti*, new edition, New Jersey, 1982, p. 73.

very unlike the little bronze Moses whose photograph Jones sent to Freud. These figures travelled as far as Florence, and Ghiberti was so impressed by them that he praises Gusmin enthusiastically, as he praises no other artist but Ambrogio Lorenzetti.

But this praise, this tribute, is all that remains of Gusmin. More dramatic still, there is practically nothing left of the work of Gusmin's contemporaries, from which we can see precisely what kind of work was done in this period in the royal ateliers, in precious metal. In fact there are three or four outstanding objects in all from France in these decades. If that number seems low, compare it with an account drawn up of the whole remaining corpus of secular goldsmiths' work from medieval France, which contains around fifty items only.[14]

It is true that plate, the personal silver and gold possessions of a family or institution, both represented

14 R. W. Lightbown, *Secular Goldsmiths' Work in Medieval France: A History*, London, 1978. On the rarity of early goldsmiths' work see also the *Burlington Magazine*, June 1995, for Timothy Schroder's 'A royal Tudor rock-crystal and silver-gilt vase', which describes the only such object of any importance which can be associated with Henry VIII and which is indisputably of English manufacture. The publication of this vase brings to a total of four the surviving objects from Henry's Jewel House.

wealth and *constituted* wealth, so that it would not, in past centuries, have always seemed so shocking to melt down plate for a purpose well conceived. But Gusmin was shocked that his gold shrine was melted down, and it is shocking to think that not just individual objects but whole classes of object have disappeared. It was calculated somehow that what remains of medieval works of art represents only 2 per cent of what there once was.[15] A statistician might say that this is far too small a sample for us to use for any generalizations about medieval art. If so, the case is perhaps no worse than that of Greek tragedy. But still, the category of what has vanished is worth our attention.

Some sculpture, like the centrepieces carved in ice or butter beloved of the luxury cruises, is made to vanish. This genre has a history going back at least to the Rome of the baroque, when we are told that the food itself would be served in a sculptural context, so that there might be 'men throwing trapping-nets over already roasted partridges, or hunters shooting at the game dishes'. Jennifer Montagu writes that 'real sculpture would be moulded in butter, or

15 Gert van der Osten, cited by Jacques Baudouin in *La Sculpture flamboyante*, vol. 1, p. 46 (n.d. Paris).

cast in jelly, ice or sugar; we may note that the Germans also sculpted in turnips and beetroot, although the Italians seem to have drawn a line at this. So important was the making of these objects that a plan of the Vatican kitchens shows a special room labelled "Room in which the *trionfi* are prepared".'

These *trionfi*, these triumphs, were made largely of sugar and decorated with edible gilding. Astonishing in their elaboration, amazing in their subject-matter: drawings preserved in Stockholm show tables set for a meal where a sugar Christ falls under his cross on one plate, while on others are displayed the flagellation, the *Noli-me-tangere*, St Veronica with her veil and a Last Supper which you could literally eat for supper. Another table is devoted to angels displaying the instruments of the Passion – the cross, the crown of thorns, the sponge soaked in vinegar and so forth – tasteless subjects for a banquet setting, you might say. But when Pope Alexander VII gave a banquet for Queen Christina of Sweden, the sugar sculptures, by Ercole Ferrata, were of scenes of rape and attempted rape.[16]

Such banquets are acts of demolition – we love to

16 Jennifer Montagu, *Roman Baroque Sculpture: The Industry of Art*, London, 1989, chapter 8.

say, they *demolished* the meal – and the extravagance of the preparations was such that, in order not to let these acts of demolition pass unnoticed, the public was admitted for two days before, to admire the place-settings alone. But it is in the nature of 'triumphs' that they are made for the moment, that they will not be preserved, any more than stage sets will necessarily be preserved. So these rare sculptural commissions are expressions of transience.

But for the most part patron and artist lived under the illusion that their works were made to last. When Horace boasted that his poetic monument would be more lasting than bronze,[17] he at least shared in the idea that bronze itself was durable. And bronze is indeed durable. It is the monument that is not. The antique Roman bronze doors of the Pantheon were durable until Bernini needed bronze in huge quantity for the *baldacchino* in St Peter's.

To erect a statue is to make a bid for immortality, or for the immortality of the subject. When Freud's admirers wished to honour him on his fiftieth birthday, Jones tells us that they presented him with a medallion with his portrait on the obverse, and on the reverse a Greek design of Oedipus answering

17 *Odes*, III, 30.

the Sphinx, around which was inscribed a line from
Sophocles:

ΌΣ ΤΑ ΚΛΕΙΝ' ΑΙΝΙΓΜΑΤ ΉΙΔΗ ΚΑΙ ΚΡΑΤΙΣΤΟΣ
ΉΝ ΑΝΗΡ
(Who divined the famed riddle and was a man most
mighty)

'At the presentation of the medallion,' says Jones,
'there was a curious incident. When Freud read the
inscription he became pale and agitated and in a
strangled voice demanded to know who had thought
of it. He behaved as if he had encountered a *revenant*,
and so he had. After Federn told him that it was he
who had chosen the inscription, Freud disclosed that
as a young student at the University of Vienna he
used to stroll around the great Court inspecting the
busts of the former famous professors of the institution. He then had the fantasy, not merely of seeking
his own bust there in the future, which would not
have been anything remarkable in an ambitious student, but of it actually being inscribed with the
identical words he now saw on the medallion.' And
among Jones's posthumous kindnesses to Freud was
his presentation, in 1955, of a bust of Freud to be
erected in the Court, to which the line from Sophocles had been added. Jones says of this that 'It is a

very rare example of such a day-dream of adolescence coming true in every detail, even if it took eighty years to do so.'[18]

I take the anecdote to be true in this sense, that Freud, presented with the medallion, seeing his face in bas-relief, and turning the object to find his achievement so beautifully encapsulated as Oedipus questioning the Sphinx, with such a beautifully apt line chosen by Paul Federn – a line which Freud knew well and recognized – I take it that Freud was overwhelmed by the thought: this line should be my memorial. And I suppose that the 'unremarkable' adolescent ambition to have his bust displayed in the great Court of the University, the ambition to live for ever in this way, grafted its burning memory onto this new desire, so that Freud himself could not distinguish the memory from the will, and he was permitted to fib.

He had foreseen his own death and now he wanted to become a statue in order to survive. But, as it turns out, these statues that we have, these plucky survivors, have had to pass through all manner of danger – war, plunder, the price of bullion, fire,

---

18 Jones, op. cit., vol. 2, p. 15. The Sophocles line is from the last chorus of *Oedipus Tyrannus*.

damp, neglect, attention, piety, disrespect, excessive love. And some of them may be compared to those characters in films who, escaping with great difficulty from a series of dangers, and coming back into their homes and slamming the door behind them, and leaning, panting, eyes closed, against the door, open their eyes again to see the greatest danger of all staring them in the face.

To have lain unremarked in the Forum, until covered with vegetation and the detritus of centuries, would have been something. To have escaped the attention of those whose trade was to burn marble for lime – that was an achievement. And to be dug up with respect, and carted off to some cardinal's collection – that might tempt one to bless one's luck, until the first blow of the restorer's chisel. And again, a statue might be well restored, by a great sculptor who knew his business well, but then the taste of the day moves against restoration itself, and all the restorations have to be removed, leaving the statue slightly worse off than as found.

For taste is a great enemy of art. It was the taste for purity of form and truth to the material that took so many medieval statues – which had had a hard enough time during years of hatred and neglect

– and stripped them of their polychromy. Mazzuoli, Bernini's pupil, must have thought he had a prestigious commission when he carved the twelve apostles for Siena Cathedral. He must have thought his works would be there for good. How surprised he would have been to see that cathedral regothicized in the nineteenth century, and his masterpieces sold off as a job lot, to be re-erected in London, at the Brompton Oratory. But they had a lucky escape.

In 1413, a statue of St Christopher was donated to Notre-Dame in Paris. It was known for its exceptional height – no less than 28 feet – and it stood on the organ screen. In 1784, in the course of restoration work on the organ, a joist from the scaffolding fell on the statue, breaking its head. Because of this, the cathedral chapter ordered the complete destruction of the statue. A guide-book from 1791 refers to it in the words: 'this ridiculous monument to the taste and devotion of our fathers has just been destroyed'.[19]

The word vandalism, that useful word which we imagine must have been around since the days of the Vandals, was coined in 1794 to denote this attitude of revolutionary destructive zeal, and it is interesting

19 Baudouin, op. cit., vol. 3, p. 49.

that the enormous destruction of monuments which took place in the French Revolution gave birth at once to the opposite tendency, the desire to preserve these objects from the past, both in museums and in private collections.[20]

It was once the churches had been ransacked that their dispersed contents regained their value. It was once the monuments were desecrated that they began to be thought of as works of art. It was once the tree had fallen that the cry went up for the woodman to spare it.[21]

And what of those statues that *did* survive? You might say they were street-smart, so profound is their capacity to dissimulate, to engage, raise hopes, disappoint. Such was the lost Cupid of Michelangelo, found in a Florentine cellar and brought in triumph to the South Kensington Museum (the forerunner of the V & A), and which had never looked like a Cupid, nor indeed, in our privileged retrospect, like a Michelangelo, but which is now agreed to be a classical statue of a warrior, modified in the sixteenth

---

20 Francis Haskell, *History and its Images*, New Haven and London, 1993, chapter 9: 'The Musée des Monuments Français'.
21 'The Collecting of Medieval Works of Art' in Paul Williamson, *Medieval Sculpture and Works of Art*, the catalogue of the Thyssen-Bornemisza Collection, 1987.

century to represent Narcissus.[22] Such discoveries, such violent modifications of perception, have not ceased, and those who look into the history of our perceptions come away with the shaken understanding that they will not cease. We shall continue to be surprised, and baffled, and have our minds changed by and about these statues.

The two colossal figures of Alexander and his horse Bucephalus, which stand today in the Piazza del Quirinale in Rome, were thought by Master Gregorius to be the first mathematicians, to whom horses had been assigned 'because of the quickness of their intellects'. Previously, they had been 'two seers who arrived in Rome under Tiberius, naked, to tell the "bare truth" that the princes of the world were like horses which had yet to be mounted by a true king'. And their hands were raised as the hands of prophets are raised in warning.

The Dying Seneca in the Louvre was equipped by restorer with arms, a cloth around its waist and a missing thigh, and, appropriately for the philosopher, was placed on a stone bath 'unhollowed so that it seemed full of water, and reddened in imitation of

22 'Michelangelo's Cupid: the End of a Chapter' in John Pope Hennessy, *Essays on Italian Sculpture*, London, 1968.

blood'. And one clergyman remarked that 'If our sculptors knew how to make a comparably express-ive Christ, it could be depended on to bring tears to all Christian eyes, for the expression alone of this dying pagan excites sorrow in all who see him.'[23] But not all agreed. To some he looked like a criminal, to others like a slave, and finally a view was settled upon that this was not the dying Seneca slitting his veins, but a Roman copy of a Hellenistic statue of a fisherman. And so, many years later, he was removed from his blood-filled tub, demoted from the highest level of human achievement to your average low-life character.

Christ or criminal, philosopher or fisherman – those opposite interpretations would come as no surprise to these statues, which have lived in a climate of extremes – having been objects of horror, and subject to the intensest covetousness, smashed by the mob, raised up by the connoisseur, having been gouged out of the mountainside, dropped in the sea, dragged the length and breadth of Europe, fought over by princes, so that the great statues of Rome made a journey to the Louvre, and back, or so that

23 For these and many other examples see Francis Haskell and Nicholas Penny, *Taste and the Antique: Lure of Classical Sculpture 1500–1900*, 2nd edition, New Haven and London, 1982.

if you want to see the great bronzes of Prague you must take a trip to Sweden, or to London for the great marbles of Athens – just as Schliemann's treasure, the discovery of which made him happy, because it constituted the fulfilment of a childhood wish, Schliemann's treasure has been lost again in Germany, and found again in Russia, in our time.

And though they seem incontrovertibly solid, though they look like a matter of fact, these statues can be mere episodes in a game of Chinese whispers, sources of creative misunderstanding. The Callipygean Venus in Naples, which raises its dress to reveal its beautiful buttocks, has an eighteenth-century head which replaced a sixteenth-century restoration, to which it was nevertheless broadly faithful. The original restorer thought that the Venus, as she raised her dress, should look coquettishly over her shoulder. And this coquettish behaviour, a source of the statue's popularity, made people think of a classical story in which two peasant girls called a passer-by to judge which of them had the more beautiful buttocks. So that this statue has also been called La Bergère Grecque, and La Belle Victorieuse.

But the evidence of a single piece of ancient cutlery, a spatula, give us grounds to wonder whether the original statue did not show Venus looking straight ahead as she raised her dress, oblivious to any crowd or any judge. And that might make one think that a goddess raising her dress to reveal the beauty of her buttocks might, in some age past, have been the occasion for solemn awe. The statue might be a peasant girl, or a goddess, or a *hetaira*, a classical Geisha. And while it is a well-known failing of some men to consider women as either goddesses or prostitutes, there remained the possibility, for the Greeks, of religious prostitution, or the possibility that goddess and prostitute were not opposites.

One supposes that the *anasyrma*, the gesture of lifting the dress, is as complex a symbolic act as could be depicted. I recall that at the end of a certain war, the women of the city lifted their dresses to shame the young soldiers of the victorious army. Humiliation, invitation, various kinds of biological need, the sexual defiance of the can-can – here I am and damn your hypocrisy – one could go on for ever listing the various ways of lifting a dress.

The King of Sweden, Gustavus III, had the idea of copying the Callipygian Venus but giving it the head of one of his court beauties, Countess Ulla von Höpken, and this statue was made by Sergel and placed in the Hall of Mirrors where the King used to lunch, and where, as a shocked courtier noted, the lower functionaries of the household were wont to resort. The King no doubt felt that his affection for the Countess was appropriately expressed. The household no doubt did a great deal of sniggering.[24]

But if they sniggered, if they thought the statue obscene, they too take us back to a classical precedent of some beauty. You will recall that when Persephone was abducted by Hades, Demeter lost all her gaiety, refused all food and drink, and went wandering for nine days and nine nights, inconsolable. On the tenth day she came to Eleusis, and it was there that the lame daughter of the King, Iambe, after whom the iambic metre is named, tried to make her laugh with lascivious verses. And there was an old woman called Baubo, who tried to persuade Demeter to drink barley-water, flavoured with mint. And the old woman succeeded in the following way. She began groaning as if in labour. Then suddenly, unexpectedly, she lifted her skirt, and out jumped Demeter's own son, Iacchus, 'who leapt into his mother's arms and kissed her'. And once she had laughed, Demeter drank the barley-water – not just a cup of it, she drank the whole pitcher – and when the

24 Diary of Gustav Johan Ehrensvärd, 12 April 1780, cited in Gösta Säflund, *Aphrodite Kallipygos*, Uppsala, 1963.

King's son said, 'How greedily you drink', Demeter 'threw him a grim look, and he was metamorphosed into a lizard'.[25]

We understand that the passage of the seasons is reflected in Demeter's mourning for Persephone, and that, unless Demeter drinks that barley-water, winter will go on for ever. Unless Baubo, the old crone, manages to make Demeter laugh, civilization will cease. Everything depends on this obscene gesture, and it is said that the Eleusinian mysteries re-enacted this crucial moment, that they kept the obscenity going.

'You have to laugh.' That catch-phrase is true. I remember in Borneo, when we needed the river to rise so that we could get back downstream, our guides involved us in a rain-ceremony, in which we placed salt on the river bank at the height we wished the river to reach by the next morning. Then we were instructed to get into the river and beat it with branches and shout at it at the tops of our voices. I apologized for laughing as we did so. My guide said, No, you *must* laugh; if you do something funny you must laugh, otherwise the magic won't work.

25 Robert Graves, *The Greek Myths*, revised edition, London, 1960, vol. 1, p. 90.

I think it misleading of Freud to refer to animistic societies as displaying the omnipotence of thought. There may be that aspect to magic, but an animist also, by the very act of attributing spirit to everything, giving every element of the landscape its own point of view, shows himself alive to the fact that there are other powers in the world. Something must be done to make the river co-operate, but indeed the thing that must be done may be absurd, like giving a cigarette to a rock, or a coin to a stream. It is not a fantasy of omnipotence. It is a matter of doing your best in a difficult, hostile world.

And the world of statues, which is characterized at the start by the presence of these gods, these heroes and saints, is one in which the spectator is alive to forces of a complexity we can barely grasp. Is Aphrodite raising her dress to attract us, to amuse us, to ask for our opinion on the beauty of her buttocks? Or does she stand looking ahead, while she removes her robe? Is she simply undressing, because Aphrodite has to undress, just as we have to laugh, or the world will cease?

Freud, when his father died, began a collection of objects from the classical and pre-classical age, objects which might resemble statues, or toys, or idols of various kinds, but which for the most part come under the general rubric: grave-goods. And the people at the Kunsthistorisches Museum in Vienna did Freud the kindness of undervaluing his collection, so that on payment of a small sum he could take his valued grave-goods with him into exile and death. And the Greeks had a word for statues, they called them *agalmata*, which meant things wherein one delights; glories, delights, ornaments; statues in honour of a god, any statue or image; and a sculptor was an *agalmatopoios*, a maker of delightful things. And we know that Freud was thinking: maybe this instinctual renunciation, this hatred of images, has made us proud, has made us superior. And we believe that he perhaps felt that the punishment of the Jews had something to do with this pride. But when he saw Maresfield Gardens, and the beauty of the *garden* at Maresfield Gardens, he was moved to say *Heil Hitler*, in thanks for his good fortune. And his son unpacked his collection, and set it out on his desk. Death and delight were mingled there, among meanings and resonances we cannot hope to unravel, just as we will never unravel what all these statues mean, or what they once meant to those who de-lighted in them.

This book is the text of the 1995 Ernest Jones Lecture, given at Middlesex Hospital, London, on 1 November 1995, under the auspices of the British Psycho-analytical Society.